My
Bead Box

Gillian and
Marion Haslam

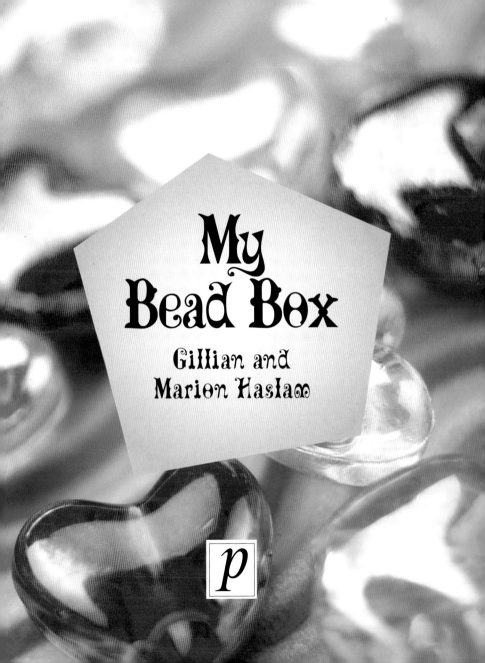

My Bead Box

Gillian and Marion Haslam

p

This is a Parragon Book

Parragon
Queen Street House
4 Queen Street
Bath BA1 1HE, UK

Copyright © Parragon 2001

Designed, produced and packaged by
Stonecastle Graphics Limited

Text by Gillian and Marion Haslam
Edited by Philip de Ste. Croix
Designed by Sue Pressley and Paul Turner
Craft items by Marion Haslam
Photography by Roddy Paine

ISBN 0-75255-683-5

Printed in China

Disclaimer:
• Beads are great fun but safety is
very important.
• Do not allow babies or young children
under five years old to play with beads
as they may swallow them.
• Keep beads away from family pets, who
could swallow one and choke.
• Beads must never be put in your mouth
or thrown about as they may cause
damage or injury.
• Do not leave beads where others may
step on them.
• Always put your beads away tidily
and safely.
The publisher and their agents cannot
accept liability for any loss, damage or
injury caused.

Contents

Introduction

Beading is such a versatile craft that you are sure to become hooked on it. This book is full of ideas for making beautiful jewellery, from bead-and-feather necklaces to dangly earrings, and from brilliant bracelets to ribbon chokers. There are also suggestions for fantastic hair decorations, such as beaded hair grips and sparkly scrunchies that you'll love to wear.

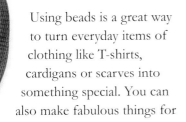

Using beads is a great way to turn everyday items of clothing like T-shirts, cardigans or scarves into something special. You can also make fabulous things for your bedroom, such as photo frames and a window decoration, and you'll never be short of great ideas for presents to make for your friends and family, using beads in many different ways.

You'll find the projects here are very simple to make and you will have loads of fun with your friends thinking up new ways to use beads after you have tried making everything in this book.

So enjoy the ideas and get beading!

The Story of Beads

Beads have been part of our history for centuries. Beads carved from bone and shell dating from as far back as 30,000BC have been discovered in France and India.

In past times they were used as currency, allowing people to trade with one another. In some countries you can tell how important or wealthy a person is by the amount of beaded jewellery they wear or the decoration on their clothes.

Beads have always been made from many different materials and they come in all colours of the rainbow. Those made from glass are very common, especially in Europe where one of the most famous centres for bead-making is Murano in Venice, Italy. In Tudor and Stuart England, valuable gemstones were often sewn onto clothes as beads. Pearls have also been used for many years, with the tiniest ones being known as seed pearls. In India and North Africa, jewellers have often used engraved beads made from metals such as silver. Nowadays, metal is often recycled so you may find beads made from old tin cans, saucepans or even bits of cars!

As well as being carved from precious stones such as amber, jade, amethyst or jet, beads are also made from more everyday materials such as clay or dried mud, which can be glazed or painted. The most unusual shapes of clay or mud beads come from Peru. In the Philippines they make beads from wood or the

husks of coconuts which are then painted in bright colours. Plastic is now widely used in bead-making to imitate precious stones; it is also moulded into all sorts of fantastic shapes, such as flowers and fruits.

Materials

Beading does not need a lot of unusual materials or equipment which makes it very easy to get started. With a selection of needles, some sharp scissors, sewing thread and a pot of craft glue, you can make all the projects shown in this book. Here we explain what everything is and how to use it.

Beads

You can find beads in many places. There are specialist bead shops which offer a great choice and many department stores also sell them – look in the haberdashery or sewing sections. You can find them in mixed packs or packets that contain just one design or colour. Also, ask friends or family for old necklaces that they no longer wear – you can undo these and reuse the beads.

Some beads have special names – you will see these on the packets when you buy them. Bugle beads are long, cylindrical beads, often used in 1920s' fashions, such as beaded "flapper" dresses. Rocaille beads are the tiny, round beads made from glass or plastic – they are great to use between larger beads to stop them bumping into each other. You can also buy lengths of beaded fringing which are ideal to use as trims on bags, clothing and jewellery. The beads are already sewn onto lengths of ribbon. This type of fringing has been used on the jewellery box on page 32 and the scarf on page 44.

Sequins

Sequins are not just small, glittery circles. Nowadays you can buy them in all sorts of shapes, sizes and colours, from silver snowflakes to gold stars and metallic flowers. You can combine them with beads and they can either be sewn or glued into place. They add a wonderful sparkle to clothing.

Shisha mirrors are another type of glittery decoration, often used in traditional Indian clothing and decorations for the home. They are formed of a tiny, round mirror about 1cm ($^1/_2$in) across, surrounded by a stitched thread border and they can be glued or sewn on.

Needles

You will need three types of needle for beadwork: everyday sewing needles, a beading needle (this is a long, slender needle with a small eye, ideal for passing thread through slender bead holes) and a darning needle for threading narrow ribbon through beads. A needle threader is handy to use with a beading needle. This makes it far easier for you to thread the needle.

Pins

These are useful for holding beads in position before they are sewn in place. It's a good idea to buy pins which are supplied in a tub with a snap-on lid – keep the lid on when you're not using them and you will not spill them all over the floor.

Scissors

If you do a lot of craft work, it's a good idea to keep one pair of scissors for cutting paper and another pair for cutting thread and fabric as this will keep both sets of blades sharp. Buy scissors with differently coloured handles so you remember which is which, or tie a tag around the handle to identify them.

Remember to take care with scissors and don't let young children get hold of them.

Glue

You will need a pot of white craft glue. This is good for sticking fabric, paper, sequins and beads and the glue dries clear. There is often a brush in the lid of the pot (although this can be a bit clumsy for fine beadwork). If you brush glue in the wrong place, leave it to dry then simply peel it off. You only need to use a little at any time. Keep the lid on the pot when you are not using it so that it does not dry out.

Cotton buds

These are great for using in gluework as a tiny brush, rather than using the larger brush supplied in the glue pot. They are just the right size for dabbing a spot of glue onto the backs of beads or sequins.

Wire

Two projects in this book use wire – the beaded wire snake on pages 30-31 and the door initial on pages 62-63. This is a special craft wire used for jewellery and beadwork and is easy to find in craft shops or the haberdashery sections of department stores. It is available in various colours (we have used silver for our projects) and different thicknesses (known as gauges) – 24 gauge is the best for these projects. You can cut it with scissors, but take care as the wire can be springy and the ends can be sharp. It may be best to ask an adult for help when cutting wire.

grips. It is perfect for fabric projects as it can be used instead of buttons or stud fasteners. You can buy it in packets as "spots" or in a length where you cut off the amount you need. Here we have used the no-sew sticky-backed variety.

Elastic

When making jewellery items such as bracelets or necklaces, thread the beads onto a length of fine shirring elastic. This elastic looks like thick sewing thread and can be used with a needle.

Velcro

Velcro is a touch-and-close fastening with two different surfaces – one has little hooks to which the other woolly surface

Basic Techniques

There's nothing difficult about mastering the art of beadcraft. All you really need is a little patience to get it right and a clear space in which to work.

It's useful to have a flat, rimmed plate onto which you can tip the beads when selecting which ones to use as this means they will not roll all over the table or spill onto the floor. When threading beads onto a needle, it's so much easier if you place the beads on a piece of felt. This stops them rolling around and you can simply "spear" the bead with the tip of the needle.

When sewing beads in place, always knot the thread first and if the beads seem at all loose, do a few extra stitches here and there and pull the thread a little tighter.

When using beads on fabric, they will stay in place far longer if you sew them on rather than gluing them. This is especially important for clothes that will be put in the washing machine.

When threading beads onto a length of thread or elastic, remember to keep hold of both ends so the beads do not slide straight off. If using plastic string, make a loose retaining knot that can be undone later. If using wire, bend the end of the wire over.

If you have younger brothers or sisters in the house, remember that beads are not toys for them to play with. This is very important as they could put them in their mouths and swallow them, or even choke on them. So don't leave beads lying around when you are not using them.

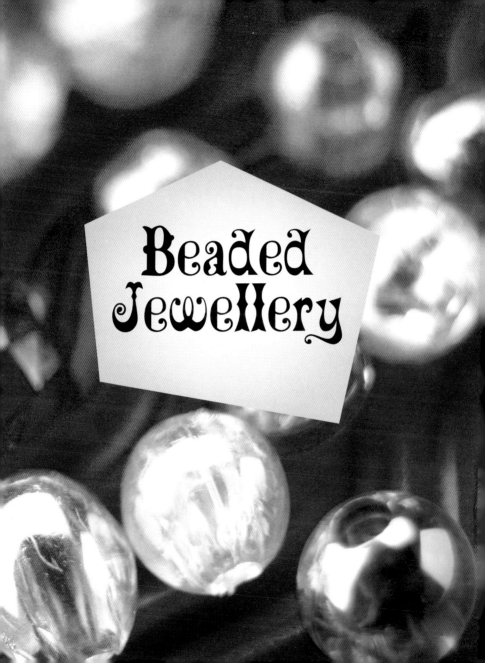

Beaded
Jewellery

Sparkly Heart Necklace

This is a great project to begin with as it's so simple and quick to make. Once you have learned how to thread beads in this way, you can make up your own designs with whatever beads you have to hand.

You will need:

- Selection of differently shaped beads
- Piece of felt
- Plastic string, about 80cm (30in) long
- Scissors

1. Lay the beads out on the piece of felt so that you can decide the order in which to thread them. Get a good mix of colours. The felt stops the beads rolling around.

2. Make a knot at one end of the string, about 5cm (2in) from the end. This will stop the beads falling off as you thread them.

3. Thread the beads on one at a time. When you get halfway, thread two hearts so they face one another, then continue as before, changing the direction of the hearts. This means that when you wear the necklace, all the hearts will point in the right direction and the two hearts next to each other will be at the bottom. Leave a 5cm (2in) length of string at the end for knotting.

4. Tie the two string ends together in a tight double knot that will not unravel. Trim off the ends of the string close to the knot.

TIPS: You'll get the best results if you use two different shapes or sizes of beads.
Here the long beads (known as bugle beads) separate the hearts and make them more noticeable.
We used plastic string, but a length of shirring elastic would work just as well.

Nature Necklace

This back-to-nature necklace uses a great selection of real wooden beads and feathers threaded onto a leather thong. The necklace can either be worn long or as a short choker.

You will need:

- Leather thong, about 70cm (28in) long
- Pack of feathers
- Three large wooden beads
- Seven small round wooden beads

1. Fold the thong in half to find the centre. Take the first feather and tie the thong around the top of the feather in a single knot. Check that the feather is in the centre of the thong.

2. Thread a small wooden bead next to the feather, then thread a large bead and follow with another small bead.

3. Tie another feather on in the same way. Thread on three more beads and fasten them in place with a single knot.

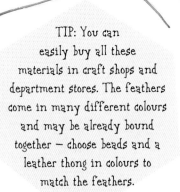

4. Repeat steps 2 and 3 on the other side of the central feather.

TIP: You can easily buy all these materials in craft shops and department stores. The feathers come in many different colours and may be already bound together — choose beads and a leather thong in colours to match the feathers.

5. When you want to wear the necklace, ask a friend to knot it behind your neck. But make sure she doesn't knot it so tightly that you can't undo it later!

Velvet Ribbon Choker

This is a perfect accessory if you are getting dressed up for a special party or disco. Choose ribbon in a colour to match your outfit. You can either sew beads all around the choker or just sew three special beads to the centre. You can also buy lengths of braid with beads already attached — you just need to sew this to your length of velvet ribbon.

1. Ask friend to measure around your neck. Add 2cm (about 1in) to this measurement and cut the ribbon to this length.

2. Sew the beads onto the velvet ribbon, leaving 3cm (1¼in) of ribbon blank at each end.

3. Peel the backing paper off one piece of the Velcro and stick to the facing side of one end of the ribbon.

4. Stick the other piece of Velcro to the reverse side of the other end of the ribbon.

Tip: The smallest amount of Velcro you can usually buy is a 10cm (4in) length. You only need a fraction of it for this choker, so save the rest for other projects in this book.

Beaded Felt Cuff

You'll find these wrist cuffs in all the fashion shops, but they are so easy to make, why not try doing it yourself? They are also great presents to give to friends, rather like friendship bracelets.

You will need:
- Piece of felt measuring 6 x 20cm (2^1/2in x 8in)
- Scissors
- White craft glue
- Selection of sequins or beads
- 1cm (^{1}/2in) of stick-and-stick Velcro
- Needle and sewing thread in a colour to match the felt

1. Fold the felt into three lengthways. Using the glue-pot brush, lightly brush the centre strip of the felt with the glue. Fold one side onto the glue and press down. Leave for a few minutes to stick.

2. Brush more glue onto the double layer of felt and fold the remaining outside edge over. The felt is now three layers thick. Leave for a few minutes to stick.

3. Thread the needle and tie a small knot in one end of the thread. Decide on the order of your beads or sequins and sew them in place. Leave the final 2.5cm (1in) of one end of felt blank.

4. Peel the backing paper off one piece of the Velcro and stick to the facing side of the end of the beaded side of the felt.

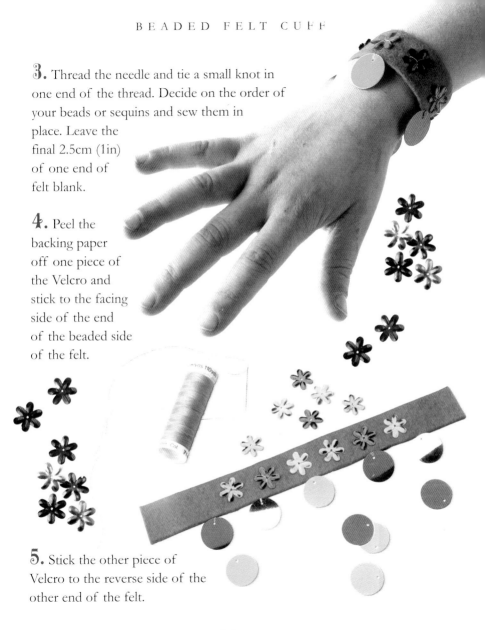

5. Stick the other piece of Velcro to the reverse side of the other end of the felt.

Dingly-Dangly Earrings

Earrings are so quick and easy to create, so make several pairs and mix and match the colours to suit your clothes. The special shaped wires are sold in multi-packs, so why not use the spares to make a present for a friend who has just had her ears pierced?

You will need:

- Selection of beads or feathers (each earring will only use a few beads)
- Piece of felt
- Two head pins
- Two silver kidney ear wires
- Small sharp scissors

1. Tip all the beads out onto the felt. The felt stops the beads rolling away and makes it easier to pick them up. Decide on the order of beads. It is a good idea to separate larger ones with small rocaille beads.

2. Spear the beads in the right order onto the head pin, leaving at least 5mm (¹/₄in) of the pin unbeaded.

3. Holding the beads and head pin in one hand to stop them sliding off, twist over the end of the head pin into a small loop. Snip off any surplus wire with the scissors. Thread the beaded head pin onto the kidney wire and pinch the small loop on the wire with your fingers so that the head pin is firmly attached.

4. Repeat with the other head pin, making sure that the beads are threaded in the same order.

TIP: If you do not have pierced ears, you can also buy earclips and earscrews instead of kidney ear wires. If you make a lot of jewellery, you may find it helpful to buy a pair of snipe-nosed jewellery pliers to help with making loops and squeezing the wires. These are available from good craft shops.

Butterfly Bracelet

This bracelet looks fab with the Sparkly Heart Necklace on page 18. It's made with narrow elastic so it's easy to slip on and off your wrist. Wearing jewellery like this is a great way to jazz up a plain outfit.

You will need:

• 45cm (18in) length of elastic
• Selection of beads, including tubes, balls and butterfly shapes
• Scissors

1. Fold the elastic in half and thread on one tubular bead. Thread one ball bead on either side of the tube.

2. Thread both ends of the elastic through another tube bead, a butterfly bead and one more tube bead.

3. Thread two ball beads onto each separate piece of elastic.

4. Repeat steps 2 and 3 until you reach the end of the elastic. Finish with a butterfly bead. Leave 4cm (1½in) blank at the end of the elastic. Thread one end of the elastic through the first tube bead and tie the two ends together in a tight double knot. Snip off the ends of elastic close to the knot.

TIP: You need a length of stretchy elastic to make this project. Alternatively, simply buy a reel of shirring elastic – it's easy to find.

Beaded Wire Snake

This eye-catching "snake" is simply made from beads threaded onto a length of craft wire. This can be curled around your arm as an exotic bracelet. This is a great way of using up leftover odds and ends of beads, or you could buy a pack of assorted beads specially for this project.

You will need:
- Selection of beads
- Piece of felt
- 1m (3ft) length of wire (see Tip)
- Scissors

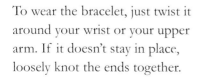

To wear the bracelet, just twist it around your wrist or your upper arm. If it doesn't stay in place, loosely knot the ends together.

1. Tip all the beads out onto the felt. The felt stops them rolling away and makes it easier to pick them up.

2. Twist over the end of the wire as shown in the photograph. This stops the beads slipping off.

TIP: Craft wire can be bought from craft shops or department stores — you will usually find it next to the beads as it is used to make jewellery. It comes in different colours and thicknesses and is sold on a reel. Here we used a 24-gauge thickness.

3. Spear the beads onto the wire in any order you like. Get a good mix of colours and shapes. From time to time, shake the wire so that the beads slide down to the bottom. Continue to the end of the wire, leaving 3cm (1 1/4in) blank.

4. Bend the wire back on itself, leaving a tiny loop at the end (to stop the beads falling off) and make a couple of twists around the base of the loop. Using scissors, snip off the end of the wire.

SAFETY TIP: Take care when making this project as the ends of the wire can be sharp. Make sure you keep them away from your eyes. You may need to ask an adult to help cut the wire for you.

Bejewelled Box

When you have made all your beaded jewellery, you will need somewhere to store it. This box is the perfect answer. You can either buy a box from a stationery store or re-use one of those smart boxes that special chocolates often come in.

You will need:

- Cardboard box with a lid
- Sheet of paper and a pencil
- Scissors
- Selection of flat beads
- White craft glue
- Cotton buds
- Length of beaded fringing, long enough to go right around the lid with a slight overlap

1. Cut the piece of paper to the same size as the box lid. In pencil, draw your initial. Place the paper on top of the lid, then trace over the initial again, pressing hard, to create an indentation on the box lid.

2. Position the beads on the lid. When you are happy with the arrangement, use the cotton bud to add a dab of glue to the back of a bead and press it into position on the lid. Continue with all the beads. Leave to dry thoroughly.

3. Use a clean cotton bud to brush a thin line of glue around the edge of the box lid. Carefully stick the beaded fringing into place and leave it to dry again.

Tip: Wrap your items of jewellery individually in pieces of tissue paper before placing them in the box so that the beads do not get tangled up.

Beads to Wear

Flower Power Spaghetti Top

Sparkle in the summer with these funky flowers. You could use this idea on any T-shirt or jumper. As well as beads, we used shisha mirrors which are often seen on traditional Indian costumes. They can be bought in craft shops and department stores.

You will need:

- Spaghetti top
- Five shisha mirrors
- 35 bugle beads
- Pins
- Needle and sewing thread in a colour to match the top

1. Position the shisha mirrors on the front of the top and pin them in place. Remember to allow enough space around them for the bugle beads. Starting with the top row, stitch the shisha mirrors in place.

2. Working one flower at a time, sew on the beads. Bring the needle up at the edge of the mirror, thread through the bead and take to the back of the T-shirt. Bring the needle out again further round the mirror, ready to sew the next bead. Sew seven beads around each flower, mixing up the colours. Knot and cut off the thread and start on the next flower.

TIPS: It's important to keep the thread taut when stitching on the beads. However, don't pull too tightly or you will wrinkle the T-shirt. When sewing on the beads, make sure that you only stitch through the front of the T-shirt — don't stitch right through to the back or you will not be able to get it over your head later on!

Cool Cardigan

You'll feel really grown-up in this pretty cardigan with its decorated front edges and cuffs. It's great for special occasions and is really easy to sew. We used the beads illustrated, but pearls or other sparkly beads would work just as well. You could even stitch sequins between the beads.

You will need:
- Cotton cardigan
- Selection of beads
- Pins
- Needle and sewing thread in a colour to match the cardigan

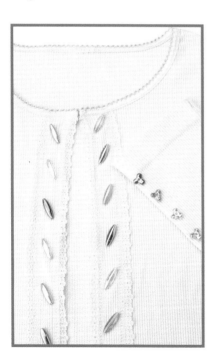

1. Lay the cardigan on a flat surface. Place the beads in position along the front edges. Make sure that they are evenly spaced. Mark the position of each bead with a pin. Remove the beads.

2. Thread the needle and knot the thread at one end. Starting at the top, sew on the first bead. Bring the thread through from the back of the cardigan, pass the needle through the bead and take the needle to the back of the cardigan. Repeat this twice so the bead is firmly attached, than pass the needle down to the next pinned position. Sew on the rest of the beads in the same way.

3. To decorate the cuffs, mark the position of the beads as in step 1 and stitch in place as in step 2.

TIP: For the best results, choose a cardigan that does not button up, as buttonholes would interfere with the design. We used beads that look like small buttons for the cuffs, but you could use the same beads as on the front if you wish.

Fun in the Sun Flip-Flops

B e the smartest girl on the beach. Brighten up your flip-flops with beautiful beads and stunning sequins, and add a matching ankle bracelet for the perfect finishing touch.

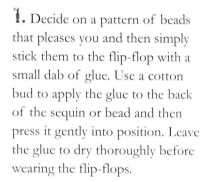

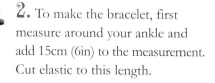

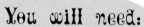

You will need:

- Pair of flip-flops
- Beads or sequins
- White craft glue
- Cotton bud
- Tape measure
- Shirring elastic
- Scissors

1. Decide on a pattern of beads that pleases you and then simply stick them to the flip-flop with a small dab of glue. Use a cotton bud to apply the glue to the back of the sequin or bead and then press it gently into position. Leave the glue to dry thoroughly before wearing the flip-flops.

2. To make the bracelet, first measure around your ankle and add 15cm (6in) to the measurement. Cut elastic to this length.

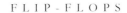

3. Hold one end of the shirring elastic in one hand and thread the beads on to the other end. When you have threaded 20-25 beads, place the bracelet around your ankle, pull the elastic a little tighter and tie the ends in a double knot. Trim the ends of the elastic close to the knot.

Tip: We used coloured artificial seashell beads, but you could make this with real, small seashells collected from the beach. You may even find some with holes already worn in them.

41

Hippy Chic Satchel

This bag is just the right size for carrying all those important bits and bobs around. We decorated a bag bought from a shop, but you could easily make a bag from a rectangle of fabric with a length of cord added for the strap.

You will need:
- A small shoulder bag
- Shisha mirrors
- Beads
- Needle and sewing thread to match the colour of the bag

1. Arrange the beads and mirrors on the bag in a nice pattern. Here we placed them in stripes to match the look of the bag, but you can choose your own design.

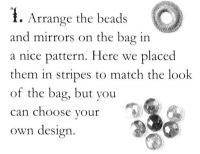

2. Thread the needle and knot the thread securely at one end. Bring the needle through from the back of the fabric (you may need to make a couple of stitches to ensure the thread doesn't pull through). Working a row at a time, stitch the shisha mirrors in place first, then sew a bead on top. Make sure you only stitch through one layer of the bag.

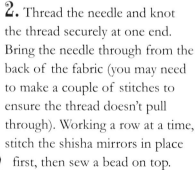

TIP: If you wish, you could thread beads onto the tassels on the base of the bag, or stitch beads along the shoulder strap.

Cosy Snowflake Scarf

Great as winter warmers, fleece scarves can easily be personalized with beads and sequins to make them really special. This scarf has been decorated with snowflake sequins and a length of ready-made beaded fringe.

1. Cut the length of fringe in half and pin to the reverse side of the short ends of the scarf. Sew in place with neat running stitches.

2. Stitch the snowflake sequins randomly along the length of the scarf on the right side, with more at each end as these are the most visible parts of the scarf when it is worn. Each sequin is attached with a couple of stitches.

You will need:
- Fleece scarf or 20cm (8in) of fleece material
- Scissors
- 40cm (16in) of beaded fringe
- Pins
- Needle and sewing thread in a colour to match the scarf
- Snowflake sequins

4 4

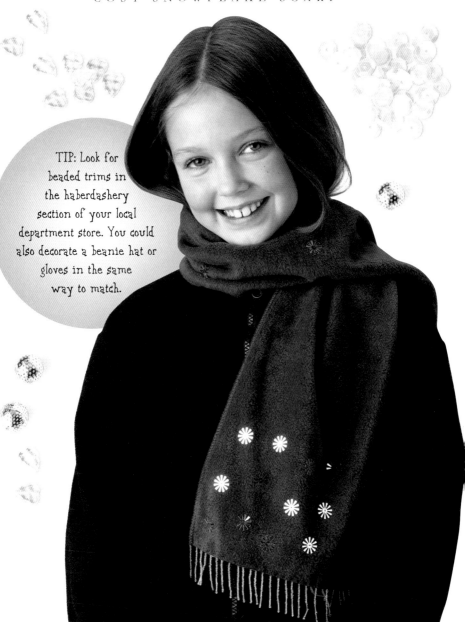

TIP: Look for beaded trims in the haberdashery section of your local department store. You could also decorate a beanie hat or gloves in the same way to match.

Beaded Hair Grips

Have you ever wished you could have your hair braided and beaded? Well, here's a much quicker and easier variation that looks just as striking. Use the narrowest ribbon you can find for this project.

You will need:

- Hair slides or hair grips
- Lengths of 3mm (¹/8in) wide ribbon
- Scissors
- Selection of beads

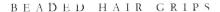

1. Cut the ribbon into lengths of 40-50cm (16-20in). If you cut the ends of the ribbon diagonally, they will not fray as easily. Thread two or three beads onto each end and secure with a double knot. Pull the beads down gently to make sure they cannot fall off the ribbon. If they seem loose, tie another larger knot.

2. Fold the ribbon in half and loop it through the hair grip, threading the ribbon ends back through the loop to secure.

TIPS: Vary the lengths of ribbon and wear several slides or grips in your hair at once for maximum effect.

• If you are using the heart or butterfly beads, make sure they will hang the right way up when the ribbon is threaded onto the slide.

Glittery Heart T-Shirt

Jazz up a plain T-shirt with some sparkly sequins. Instead of a heart, you could sew another design like a butterfly, flower or your own initial.

1. Fold the sheet of paper in half. Draw half a heart as shown, against the fold of the paper. With the paper folded, cut out the heart shape. This produces a symmetrical pattern when you open up the paper. If the shape isn't quite right, fold it in half again and trim it carefully with the scissors.

2. Fold the T-shirt to find the centre. Place the paper heart in the centre and pin it in place. Take care not to move the template.

3. Thread the needle and make a knot at one end of the thread. Starting at the bottom point of the heart, sew on the first sequin, just outside the edge of the template. Bring the needle through from the reverse side of the T-shirt and thread it through the centre hole of the sequin. Pass the needle back to the reverse side and back through the centre. Do this three times for each sequin. The last time, move your needle up about 2cm (³/₄in) away from the first sequin. Sew on the second sequin in the same way and continue to do this until the heart is finished.

4. If you wish, add a row of sequins around the bottom edge of the T-shirt and around the cuffs.

TIP: When you get near to the end of the thread, pass the needle through to the reverse side and take a couple of small stitches in the same place to secure the thread.

Cool Hairband

It's easy to find these plain fabric-covered hairbands in the shops. Make yours extra-special with twinkling beads and decorate a matching scrunchie.

You will need:
- Fabric-covered hairband
- Pack of assorted small silver beads
- Piece of felt
- Beading needle and sewing thread to match the hairband
- Needle threader
- Scissors

1. Tip the beads out onto the felt to stop them rolling away and to help you pick them up with the needle more easily.

2. Thread the needle. You will need to use a needle threader for this as the eye of the needle is very small. Tie a knot in the end of the thread. Starting a couple of centimetres (about an inch) from one end, bring the needle through to the front of the fabric and gently pull the thread.

3. Thread on the beads by spearing four or five on the point of the needle and then let them fall to the end of the thread.

4. Take a couple of stitches through the fabric of the hairband, pulling the thread tightly, and then thread more beads on as in step 2. Continue along the hairband – here we stitched them in a zigzag pattern. Finish the beading a couple of centimetres from the end of the hairband and secure the thread with a couple of stitches.

5. To make the scrunchie, pick up three or four beads on the needle in the same way and stitch randomly over the scrunchie, pulling the thread tightly so that the beads stand up.

TIP: As this project uses very small beads, use a beading needle rather than an ordinary needle. A beading needle has a far smaller eye and will therefore pass through the holes of the beads more easily.

Beads for Your Bedroom

Fantastic Photo Frames

Display your favourite photos of friends, family and pets in these jazzy frames. They also make perfect presents for special friends and relations.

You will need:
- Photo frame with a wide, flat border
- White craft glue
- Cotton bud
- Beads and sequins
- Gold or silver metallic pen

1. If using just beads or sequins, first decide where to place them. When the arrangement looks good, lift up one bead or sequin at a time. Using a cotton bud, add a small dab of glue to the back and replace the bead or sequin on the frame, pressing it securely into place. Carefully work around the frame until all are stuck in position. Lie the frame flat until the glue is thoroughly dry.

2. If using the metallic pen (as on the green frame illustrated), first decide where you want the butterfly beads to appear by placing them on the frame. Carefully lift the beads from the frame and place them on the tabletop just outside the frame. Draw the swirling motif on the frame (you

may wish to practise this first on a piece of paper). Allow the ink to dry for a couple of minutes, then stick the beads on as described in step 1.

TIPS: If using the metallic pen, it is easier to draw swirls and curls rather than straight lines.
• For best results, choose frames with a wide, flat border, ideally made from resin or plastic.

Wonderful Window Curtain

This is a great way to hide an ugly view from your bedroom window. As sunlight shining through the glass catches the beads, it makes them sparkle.

You will need:

- Tape measure
- Length of wooden dowel, the width of your window
- Scissors
- Long length of 9mm (1/3in) wide ribbon (steps 1 and 2 explain how much you will need)
- Beads
- Darning needle
- 50cm (20in) length of narrow ribbon

1. Measure the height and width of your window and note the measurements down on a piece of paper. Ask an adult to cut a length of wooden dowel slightly narrower than the window width. Put a pencil mark every 5cm (2in) along the dowel – this will tell you how many bead strings you need to make.

2. Cut a length of 9mm (1/3in) wide ribbon the height of the window plus 10cm (4in) extra. Thread onto the darning needle. Thread on the first bead, leaving a tail of 5cm (2in).

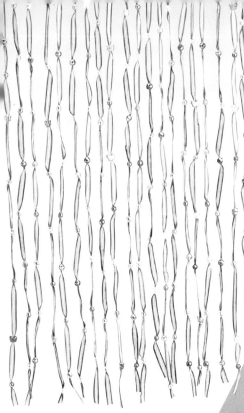

4. Tie the ribbons onto the dowel at the pencil marks, knotting them securely.

5. Cut the short length of narrow ribbon in half. Tie one end of the ribbon around one end of the dowel and ask an adult to tie the other end around the curtain rail. Repeat this for the other end of the dowel, and your bead curtain will hang at the window.

TIPS: Dowel is a lightweight wooden rod. You can buy it at DIY stores or hardware shops where they may even cut it to the size you need.
• As a variation, thread beads onto long lengths of ribbon, using a darning needle, and separate the beads with short lengths of coloured plastic straws. Tie to the dowel and attach to the curtain rail as in step 5.

3. Thread on another bead, and so on leaving a gap of about 8cm (3in) between beads until you get to within 10cm (4in) of the end of the thread, finishing with a bead. Make enough beaded ribbons to fill the width of the dowel. The beads will not slip down the length of the ribbon as it is wide enough to hold them in place.

Drawstring Treasure Bag

These bags are great for storing special things, such as scrunchies, hair slides and make-up, or they can even be used as a present sack. We chose ready-made bags in a check fabric which made it easy to position the beads.

You will need:

- Small bag with a cord drawstring
- Selection of beads (including some with a large hole for threading onto the cord)
- Needle and sewing thread in a colour to match the fabric
- Scissors

1. Decide where you want to place the beads. Thread the needle and tie a knot at one end. Starting at the bottom edge, bring the needle through from the back of the fabric to the front and sew the beads in place, using a double stitch through each bead. Continue sewing beads up as far as the drawstring.

2. Stitch a row of beads around the top of the bag in the same way.

3. Carefully untie the cord drawstring, thread on a few beads and re-knot it securely.

TIPS: Don't sew the beads too close to the drawstring as opening and closing the bag may cause the beads to work loose.
• Make sure you only sew through one thickness of the fabric.

Beaded Bookmark

There is no need to keep a beady eye on the page numbers as you read when you have this fun bookmark to keep your place. This project is ideal for using odd beads left over from other projects or for special ceramic or metal beads which you can buy singly in bead shops.

You will need

- Square of felt 20 x 20cm (8 x 8in)
- 60cm (24in) length of 3mm (^{1}/8in) ribbon
- Four beads
- Hole punch
- Scissors

1. Cut a rectangle of felt measuring 4 x 20cm (1^1/2 x 8in) and punch a hole at one end in the centre.

2. Make a double knot close to one end of the ribbon. Thread on a bead making sure it cannot pass over the knot. Leave a gap of about 4cm (1^1/2in), then make another knot and thread on two more beads. Make a third knot about 7cm (2^3/4in) from the other end of the ribbon. Thread on a fourth bead and make

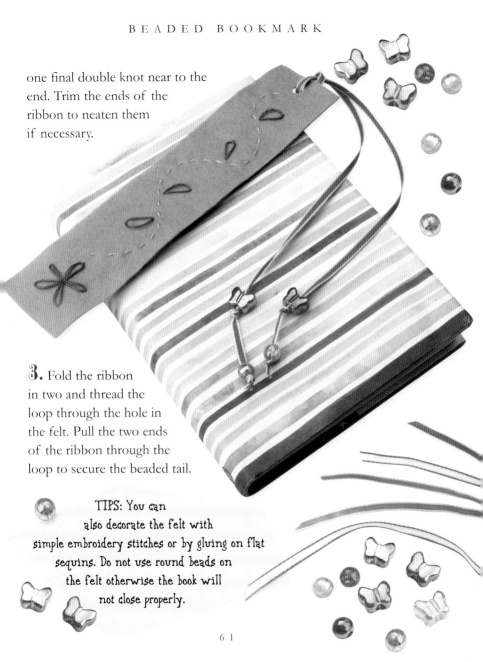

one final double knot near to the
end. Trim the ends of the
ribbon to neaten them
if necessary.

3. Fold the ribbon
in two and thread the
loop through the hole in
the felt. Pull the two ends
of the ribbon through the
loop to secure the beaded tail.

TIPS: You can
also decorate the felt with
simple embroidery stitches or by gluing on flat
sequins. Do not use round beads on
the felt otherwise the book will
not close properly.

Dazzling Door Decorations

These pretty beaded letters are just the thing to put on your bedroom door to show that it's your room. Hang them on a loop of ribbon over the door handle.

You will need:

- A4 sheet of paper
- Pencil
- Selection of beads
- Piece of felt
- 1m (3ft) length of wire
- Scissors
- 50cm (20in) length of ribbon for hanging up the initial

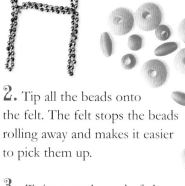

1. Draw your letter at the correct size on the paper, making the letter about 10cm (4in) in height. Depending on the initial you have chosen, it is often easier to draw a capital letter.

2. Tip all the beads onto the felt. The felt stops the beads rolling away and makes it easier to pick them up.

3. Twist over the end of the wire. This stops the beads slipping off. The wire has been cut longer than you need so that it is easier to bend it into the letter shape later. Spear the beads onto the wire in any order you like. Get a good mix of colours and shapes.

4. When you have a long enough piece of beaded wire, twist it to form the letter that you have drawn by laying it over the letter drawn on the paper. If it is not long enough, simply add more beads. Once you have made the shape of the letter, bend the end of the wire back on itself or twist around the end beads – this stops the beads falling off.

5. Loop the initial onto the length of ribbon, knot this into a loop and hang it over the door handle. Alternatively, tie it onto a longer length of ribbon and ask an adult to hang it over the top of the door.

TIPS: If you are using very tiny rocaille or bugle beads, it may be better to make the letter out of a double loop of wire so it is more noticeable. Using a double loop also makes some letters easier to shape.

• If you have a short name, make each letter in a different type of bead and then wire the letters together. Attach the ribbon to the first and last letters in order to hang up the decoration.

Acknowledgements

Many thanks to Offray Ribbons and Gutermann for supplying ribbons and beads for photography.

Useful Addresses

The Beadworkers' Guild
PO Box 24922
London SE23 3WS
Specialist society for everyone interested
in beadcraft.

The Bead Shop
21a Tower Street
Covent Garden
London WC2H 9NS
tel 020 7240 0931
Catalogue and mail order available. The shop
sells loose beads and jewellery findings.

Claire's Accessories
tel 0121 682 8000 for local branches
Great for hair accessories and small items
to decorate.

Creative Beadcraft
20 Beak Street
London W1R 3HA
tel 020 7629 9964
Catalogue and mail order available. The shop
sells loose beads and jewellery findings.

Earring Things
Craft Workshops
South Pier Road
Ellesmere Port
Cheshire CH65 4FW
tel 0151 356 4444
Catalogue and mail order available. The shop
sells loose beads and jewellery findings.
www.beadmaster.com

H & M
tel 020 7323 2211 for local branches
A good selection of clothes and accessories
to decorate.

John Lewis department stores
tel 020 7629 7711 for local branches
A good selection of beads, wire, felt, ribbons,
thread and glue is available in their
haberdashery department.

Offray Ribbons
tel 0118 973 5196 for local stockists
Manufacturers of ribbons.

Perivale-Gutermann
tel 020 8998 5000 for local stockists
Manufacturers of beads, sequins and
jewellery findings.

Also look in craft shops and the haberdashery
sections of department stores for beads,
sequins and ribbons.

Here are some useful websites for bead
stockists and enthusiasts in the UK and USA:

www.beadandbutton.com
www.beadshop.com
www.bead-patterns.com
www.beadstore.com
www.shipwreck.com
www.nationalbeadsociety.com
www.2beadornot2bead.com